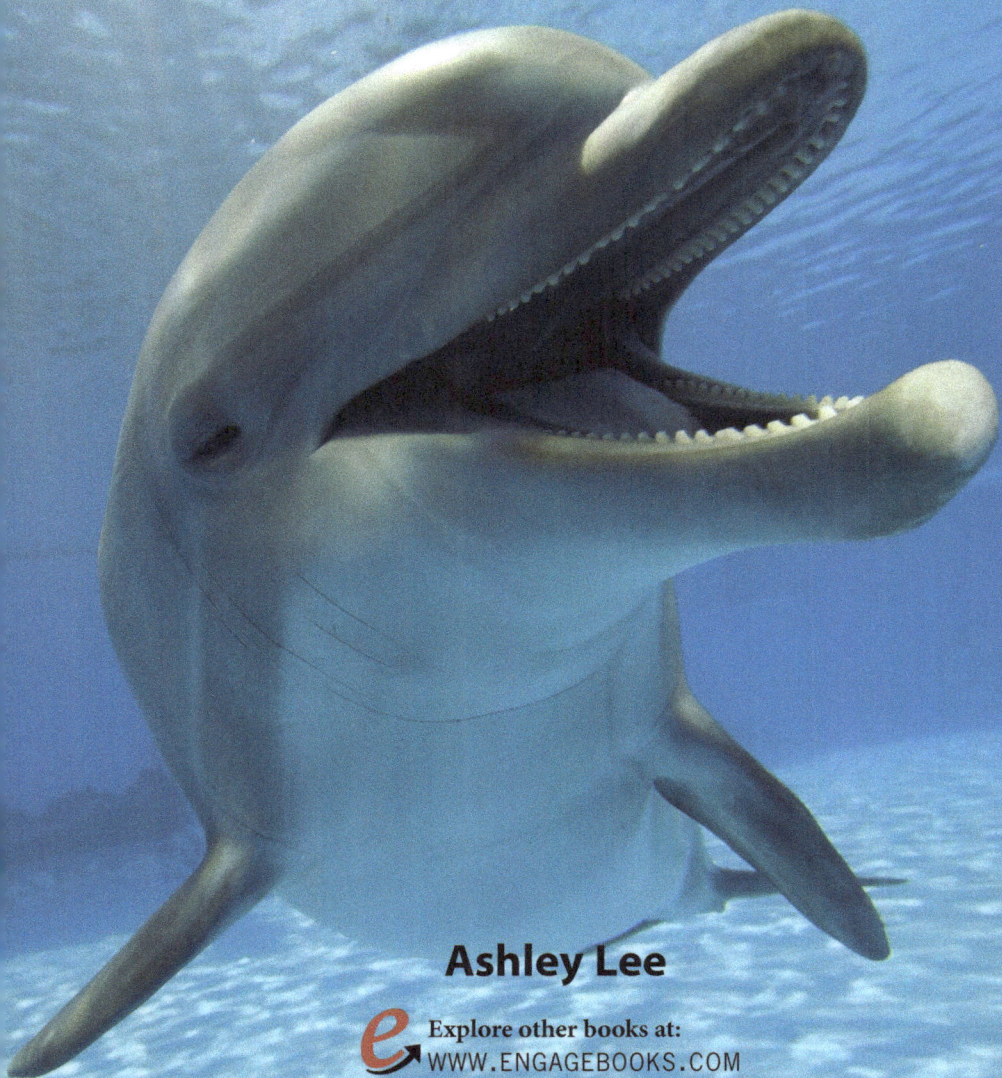

ANIMALS
That Make a Difference!

Dolphins

Ashley Lee

Explore other books at:
WWW.ENGAGEBOOKS.COM

VANCOUVER, B.C.

e → WWW.ENGAGEBOOKS.COM

Dolphins: Level 1
Animals That Make a Difference!
Lee, Ashley 1995 –
Text © 2021 Engage Books

Edited by: A.R. Roumanis
and Lauren Dick

Text set in Arial Regular.
Chapter headings set in Arial Black.

FIRST EDITION / FIRST PRINTING

LIBRARY AND ARCHIVES CANADA CATALOGUING IN PUBLICATION

Title: Animals That Make a Difference: Dolphins Level 1
Names: Lee, Ashley, author.

Identifiers: Canadiana (print) 20200309668 | Canadiana (ebook) 20200309676
ISBN 978-1-77437-687-4 (hardcover)
ISBN 978-1-77437-688-1 (softcover)
ISBN 978-1-77437-689-8 (pdf)
ISBN 978-1-77437-690-4 (epub)
ISBN 978-1-77437-691-1 (kindle)

Subjects:
LCSH: Dolphins—Juvenile literature
LCSH: Human-animal relationships—Juvenile literature

Classification: LCC QL737.C432 .L44 2020 | DDC J599.53—DC23

Contents

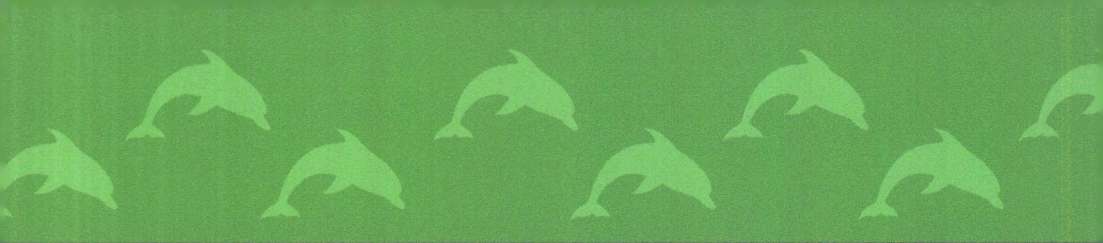

What Are Dolphins?

Dolphins are small whales with long noses.

Dolphins live in groups called pods.

What Do Dolphins Look Like?

The smallest dolphins are Maui dolphins. They are only 5 feet (1.5 meters) long. The largest dolphins are orcas. They can be up to 30 feet (9 meters) long.

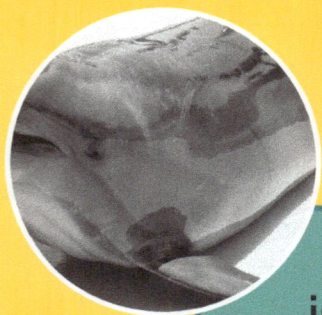

Dolphin skin is smooth. It feels like rubber.

Dolphins have a hole on the top of their heads called a blowhole. The blowhole is used for breathing.

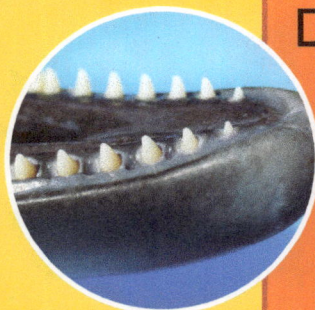

Dolphins have sharp teeth. They have between four and 240 teeth.

Where Do Dolphins Live?

Dolphins live in shallow water. They need to be able to stick their blowholes out of the water to breathe. Dolphins live in every ocean in the world. Some dolphins live in rivers.

Hector's dolphins only live near New Zealand. Burrunan dolphins live near the Australian coast. Humpback dolphins can be found near South Africa.

Arctic Ocean

South Africa

Asia

New Zealand

Africa

Pacific Ocean

Atlantic Ocean

Australia

Australian coast

| 0 | 2,000 miles |
| 0 | 4,000 kilometers |

N

Legend
☐ Land
☐ Ocean

Southern Ocean

Antarctica

What Do Dolphins Eat?

Dolphins eat fish and squid.

Large dolphins eat sea lions or smaller dolphins.

How Do Dolphins Talk to Each Other?

Dolphins talk using clicks, squeaks, and whistles. Every dolphin has a unique whistle.

Dolphins find each other using special calls. These calls bounce back to the dolphin when they hit an object. Dolphins hear their calls and can tell where other dolphins are. This is called echolocation.

Dolphin Life Cycle

Baby dolphins are called calves. They have darker skin than adult dolphins.

Calves can travel far with their mother's help. They help them until the calves become strong swimmers.

Calves live with their mothers for 3 to 6 years. Some dolphins will stay in the same pod their whole lives.

Most dolphins live for about 30 years. Some dolphins can live for more than 50 years.

Curious Facts About Dolphins

Dolphins have friends. They prefer to spend time with some dolphins more than others.

Dolphins use tools. They will cover their nose with a sponge while they search the ocean floor for food.

Dolphins can jump 20 feet (6 meters) out of the water.

Dolphins do not chew their food. They use their teeth to catch fish and swallow them whole.

Some pods are made up of more than 1,000 dolphins. Pods this large are called superpods.

Dolphins are very smart. They can solve problems and plan for the future.

17

Kinds of Dolphins

Dolphins are related to whales and porpoises. There are about 40 kinds of dolphins. They can be many different colors and sizes.

Bottlenose dolphins are one of the most common kinds of dolphins. They shed and regrow their skin every two hours.

Orcas are the largest dolphins. They are also called killer whales.

Amazon river dolphins have long snouts. Some of the males are pink.

How Dolphins Help Earth

Dolphins are a sign to humans that an area is clean and healthy. Dolphins will disappear from an area if something is not right.

Scientists know that a habitat is in danger if dolphins disappear from it. This can help scientists keep Earth clean and safe.

How Dolphins Help Other Animals

Dolphins help animals that are hurt. They will help injured animals to the surface of the water for air.

Dolphins keep oceans healthy by eating sick fish. This prevents diseases from being spread to other fish.

How Dolphins Help Humans

Dolphins have been known to save humans from shark attacks. They will also find help for people who are trapped in the water.

Some dolphins help people catch fish. They guide fish towards fishing boat nets. They are rewarded by eating any fish that escape the nets.

Dolphins in Danger

Many dolphins can get stuck in fishing nets.

This can injure the dolphins. It also stops them from getting to the surface of the water to breathe.

How To Help Dolphins

Dolphins eat garbage they find in the water. This can make them very sick.

Many people are cleaning up oceans and rivers to help save dolphins. They are cleaning up garbage and old fishing nets that can hurt dolphins.

Quiz

Test your knowledge of dolphins by answering the following questions. The questions are based on what you have read in this book. The answers are listed on the bottom of the next page.

1 Where do dolphins live?

2 How do dolphins talk?

3 What are baby dolphins called?

4 How far out of the water can dolphins jump?

5 How many kinds of dolphins are there?

6 How do dolphins keep oceans healthy?

Explore other books in the Animals That Make a Difference series.

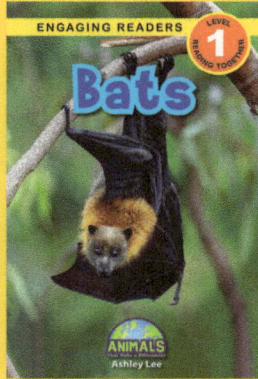

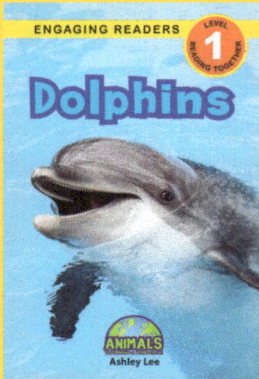

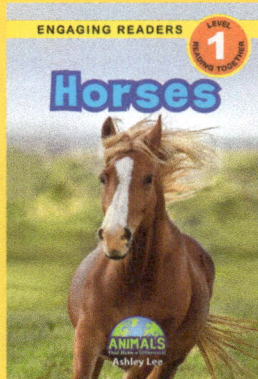

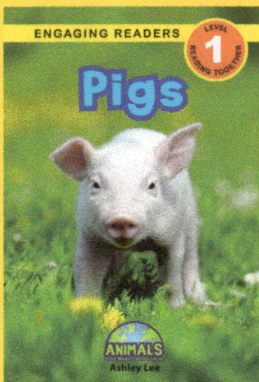

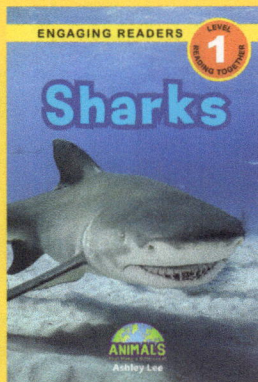

Bees
ENGAGING READERS — LEVEL 1 — READING TOGETHER
Jared Siemens

Bats
ENGAGING READERS — LEVEL 1 — READING TOGETHER
Ashley Lee

Birds
ENGAGING READERS — LEVEL 1 — READING TOGETHER
Ashley Lee

Dolphins
ENGAGING READERS — LEVEL 1 — READING TOGETHER
Ashley Lee

Horses
ENGAGING READERS — LEVEL 1 — READING TOGETHER
Ashley Lee

Lady Bugs
ENGAGING READERS — LEVEL 1 — READING TOGETHER
Ashley Lee

Pigs
ENGAGING READERS — LEVEL 1 — READING TOGETHER
Ashley Lee

Sharks
ENGAGING READERS — LEVEL 1 — READING TOGETHER
Ashley Lee

Squirrels
ENGAGING READERS — LEVEL 1 — READING TOGETHER
Ashley Lee

Visit www.engagebooks.com to explore more Engaging Readers.

Answers: 1. In shallow water 2. By using clicks, squeaks, and whistles 3. Calves 4. 20 feet (6 meters) 5. About 40 6. By eating sick fish

31

www.ingramcontent.com/pod-product-compliance
Lightning Source LLC
Chambersburg PA
CBHW051236020426
42331CB00016B/3394